LET'S DRAW COMICS

by Tony Tallarico

Publishers • GROSSET & DUNLAP • New York
A FILMWAYS COMPANY

TO NINA, ANTHONY, AND ELVIRA,
AND ALL COMICS FANS.

ISBN: 0-448-12514-5
Library of Congress Catalog Card Number: 76-4260
Copyright © 1976 by Tony Tallarico
All Rights Reserved.
Published simultaneously in Canada.
Printed in the United States of America.

There are many types of comic characters —

— even a **SUPER-HERO** can be funny!

Learn to draw a *super-hero* by following the steps on the next page ▷

DRAW YOUR OWN *SUPER-HERO* STORY HERE —

DRAW YOUR OWN *SUPER-HEROINE* STORY HERE —

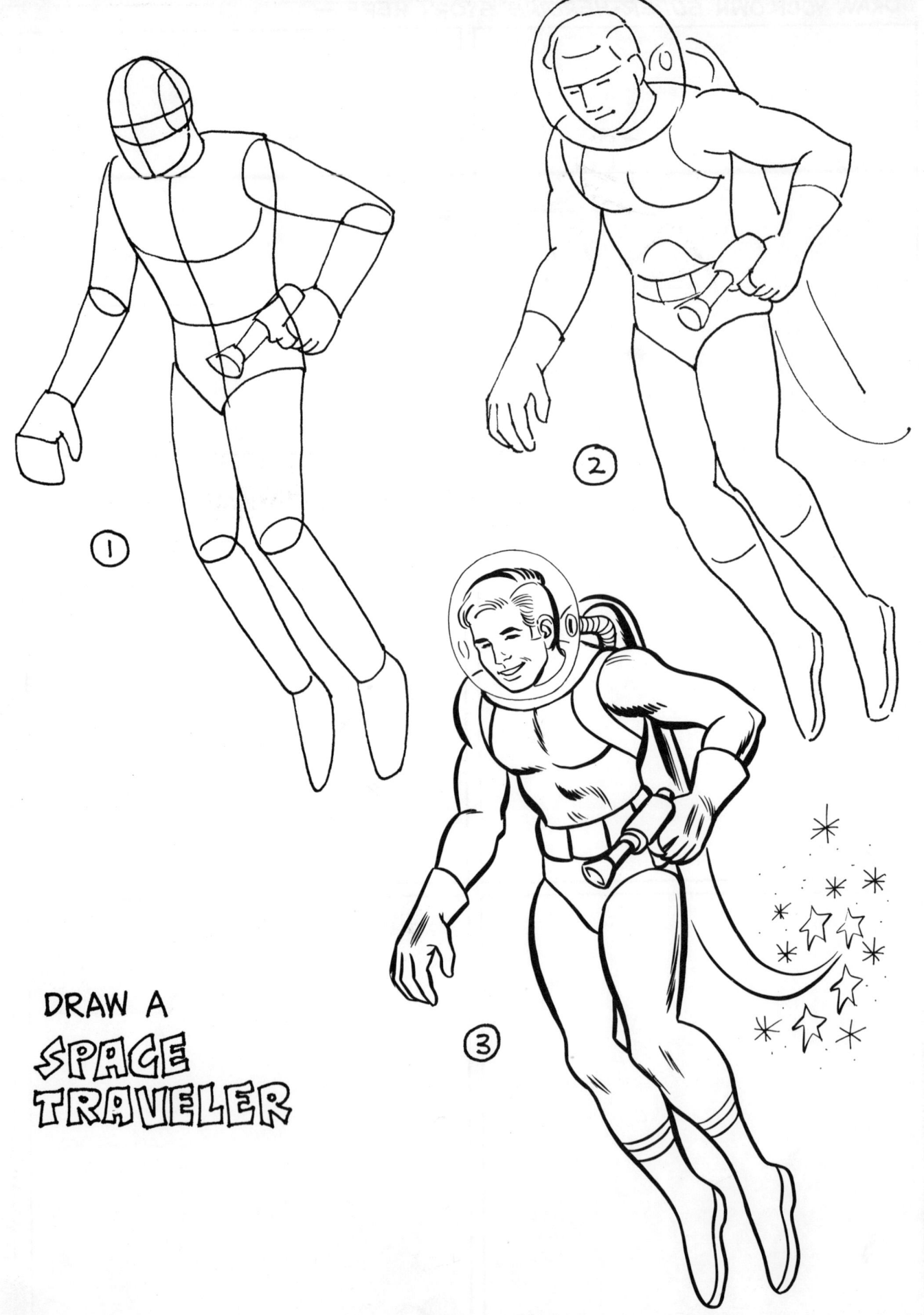

DRAW YOUR OWN *SPACE-TRAVELER* COMIC HERE –

REAL-LIFE ADVENTURE COMICS!

THESE ARE TRUE STORIES TOLD IN COMIC STORY STYLE.

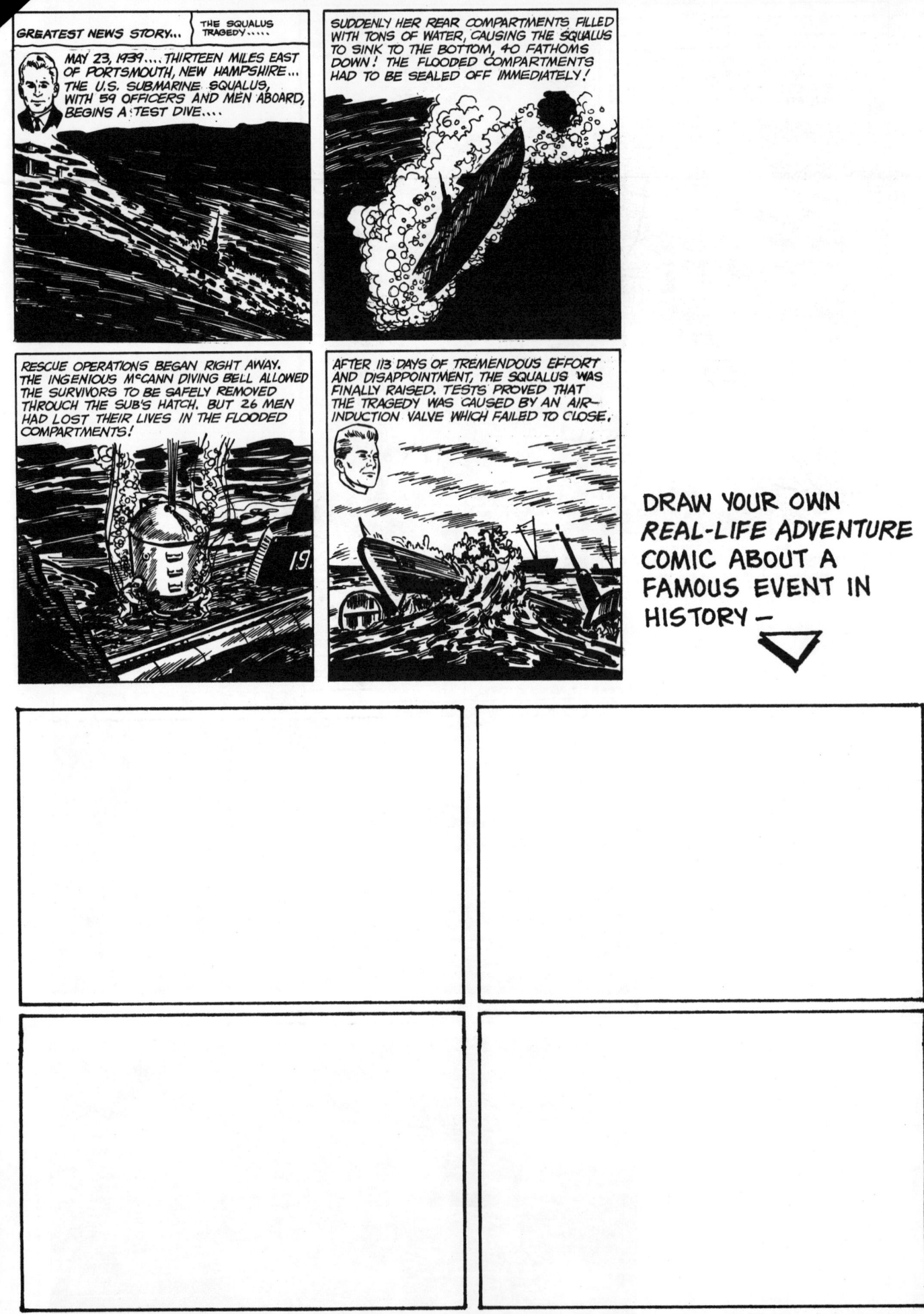

DRAWING TIPS -

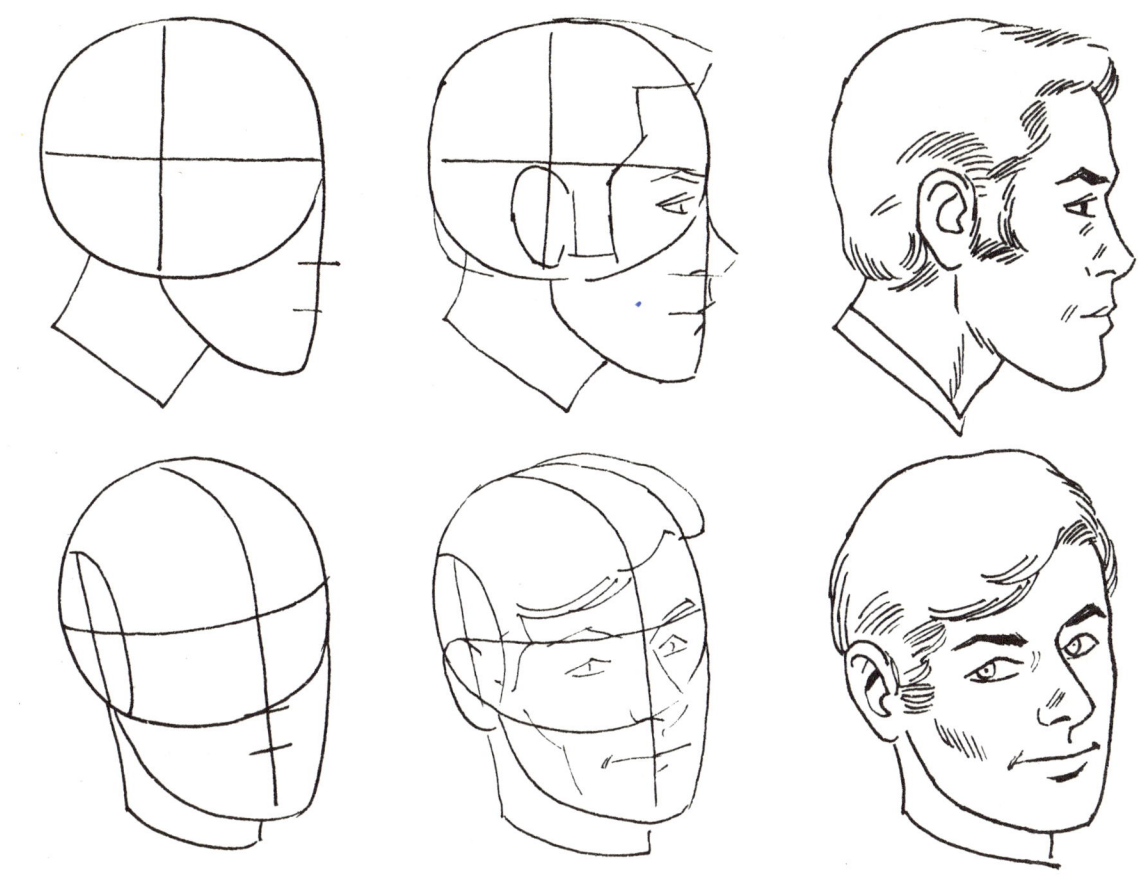

HERE ARE 6 COMIC STRIPS OF A *REAL-LIFE ADVENTURE* STORY — AFTER YOU HAVE READ THIS EXCITING STORY — TURN THE PAGE AND DRAW A *REAL-LIFE ADVENTURE* STRIP OF YOUR OWN. IT CAN BE ABOUT A FAMOUS STORY IN HISTORY OR SOMETHING THAT HAPPENED TO YOU OR A FRIEND.

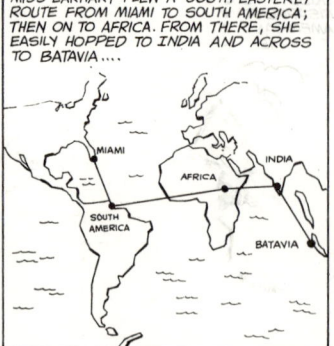

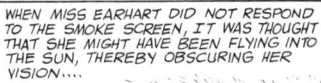

DRAWING TIPS — DRAW FIGURES IN ACTION USING THEIR BASIC SHAPES.

WHAT HAPPENS NEXT IS ENTIRELY UP TO YOU —
CONTINUE THIS STORY ON THE NEXT FEW PAGES.
- FIRST - THINK OUT WHAT'S GOING TO HAPPEN TO THE PILOT - THE GIRL - THE TWO MEN - AND DON'T FORGET ABOUT THE FLYING SAUCERS.
- THEN - WRITE OUT YOUR STORY IN THE PANELS.
- NOW - DRAW YOUR PICTURES IN THE PANELS.

DRAW YOUR OWN COMIC ON POLLUTION —

DRAW YOUR OWN COMIC ON SCHOOL—

LET'S DRAW CARTOON CHARACTERS!

CARTOON CHARACTERS COME IN MANY DIFFERENT SIZES AND SHAPES. HERE ARE JUST A FEW WAYS OF DRAWING THEM—

NOW DRAW THE TURTLES IN THIS STORY ▷

LET'S DRAW A BROTHER AND SISTER -

JACK   JILL

JACK & JILL in "TELEFUN CALL"

JACK & JILL in "FRACTION CAR"

Panel 1: "HEY, JILL! IT SAYS HERE THAT THE AVERAGE AMERICAN FAMILY HAS 1½ CARS!"

JACK IS READING THE PAPER - TALKING TO JILL.

Panel 2: "I DON'T UNDERSTAND? HOW CAN YOU HAVE A HALF A CAR?"

JACK IS PUZZLED.

Panel 3: DRAW A LARGE WORD "CRUNCH!" HERE.

Panel 4: THEY BOTH LOOK OUT WINDOW - SEE CAR THAT HAS HIT A TREE - CAR IS PUSHED IN **HALF**.

WRITE AND DRAW YOUR OWN JACK AND JILL COMICS HERE.

NOW DRAW MR. ARTT IN THIS STORY ▷

MR. ARTT

Panel 1: "I WILL NOW SCULPT A MASTERPIECE!"
MR. ARTT, HOLDING HAMMER AND CHISEL, STANDS IN FRONT OF LARGE ROCK.

Panel 2: "I GUESS I'M A REAL CUT-UP!"
HE CHISELS AWAY AT ROCK.

Panel 3: "I REALLY FEEL INSPIRED TODAY!"
STILL HAMMERING - SMALL ROCKS ON GROUND.

Panel 4: "ARE YOU FINISHED YET, DEAR?" "ALMOST, AMY, ALMOST!"
STILL HAMMERING - A GREAT MANY SMALL ROCKS ON GROUND.

Panel 5: "ALL FINISHED, AMY. A WORK OF JOY!"
FACE OF MR. ARTT

Panel 6: "GOOD! NOW TAKE ALL THOSE ROCKS ON THE GROUND OUT INTO THE BACK YARD. WE CAN START OUR ROCK GARDEN!" "good greif!"
LOTS OF ROCKS ON GROUND - HIS WIFE SPEAKS - HE LOOKS SHOCKED.

① ② ③ J.R. SMITH

① ② ③

MOM
SMITH

① ② ③ DAD
SMITH

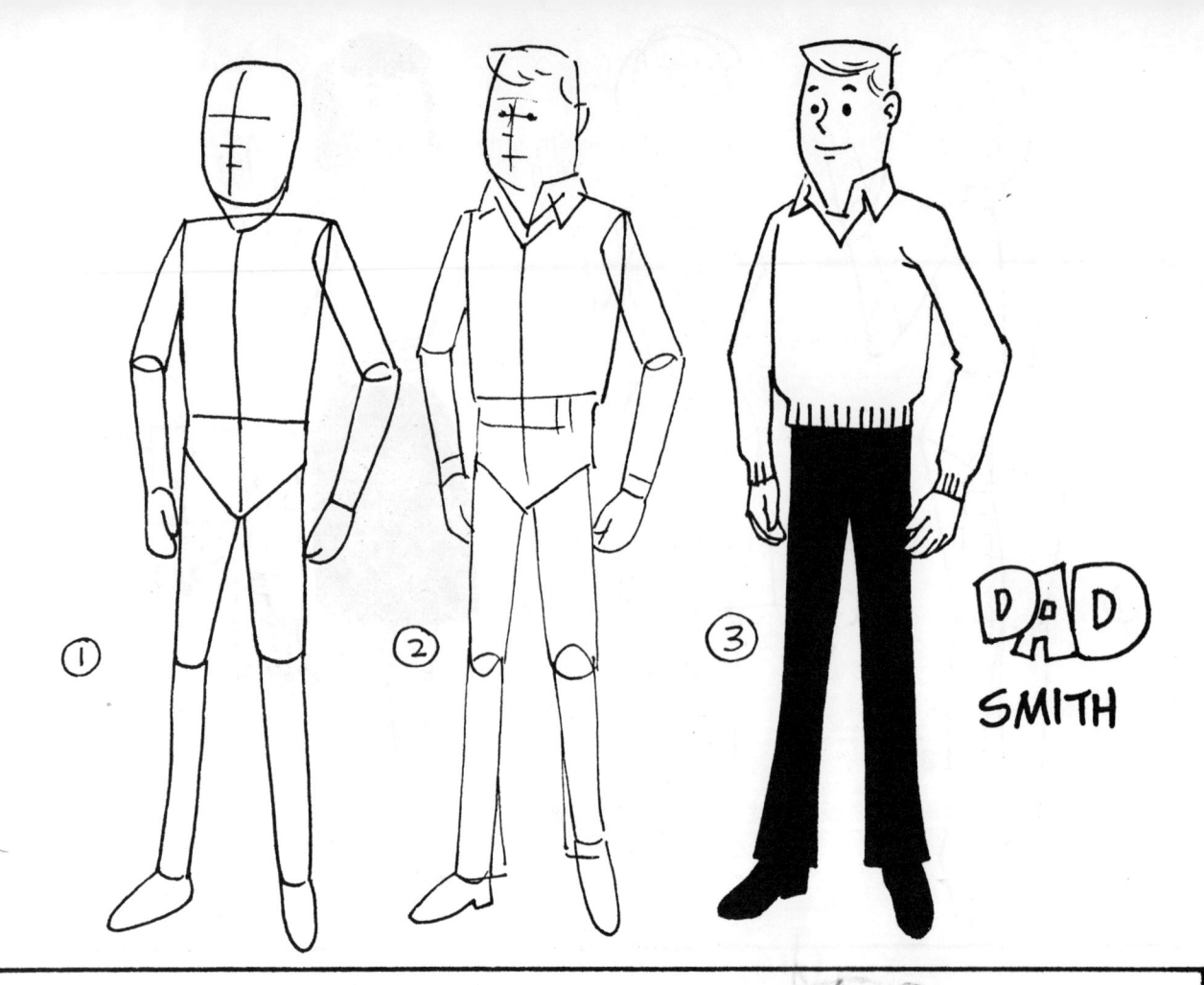

THE SMITH FAMILY

JR! GET DOWN THIS INSTANT!

YOU COULD FALL AND BREAK YOUR NECK!

WHY, YOUR FATHER AND I WOULD BE FRANTIC....

TRYING TO FIND A DOCTOR ON SUNDAY!

THE SMITH FAMILY

Panel 1: "I DON'T KNOW WHAT TO DO, JANE!"

Panel 2: "I'VE EXPLAINED AND EXPLAINED BUT IT JUST DOESN'T GET THROUGH TO JR."

Panel 3: "HE'S COMPLETELY MISSED THE POINT ABOUT THE PRESIDENTS COUNCIL ON PHYSICAL FITNESS!"

WRITE AND DRAW YOUR OWN *SMITH FAMILY COMICS* ▷

THE SMITH FAMILY   by —

THE SMITH FAMILY   by —

THE SMITH FAMILY   by —

THE SMITH FAMILY   by —

DRAW SOME LOONY SITUATIONS.

WAITIES
FOR HUSBANDS WHO ARE FOREVER WAITING FOR WIVES TO FIX THEIR BREAKFAST.

ALL-BRAWN
FOR HE-MEN AND SHE WOMEN
CONTAINS IRON, STEEL, T.N.T., SHRAPNEL, URANIUM, TIN.
BROADENS SHOULDERS AND HIPS BECAUSE FLAKES SETTLE THERE INSTEAD OF YOUR STOMACH.

SICKIES
MAKES YOU FEEL HAPPY
BETTER THAN LAUGHING GAS
IT MAY NOT TASTE GOOD - BUT YOU'LL BE TOO HAPPY TO COMPLAIN.

DRAW SOME LOONY PACKAGES.

CHAIRIOS

Racing bran

for people who want a fast start for the morning

Rice Crunches

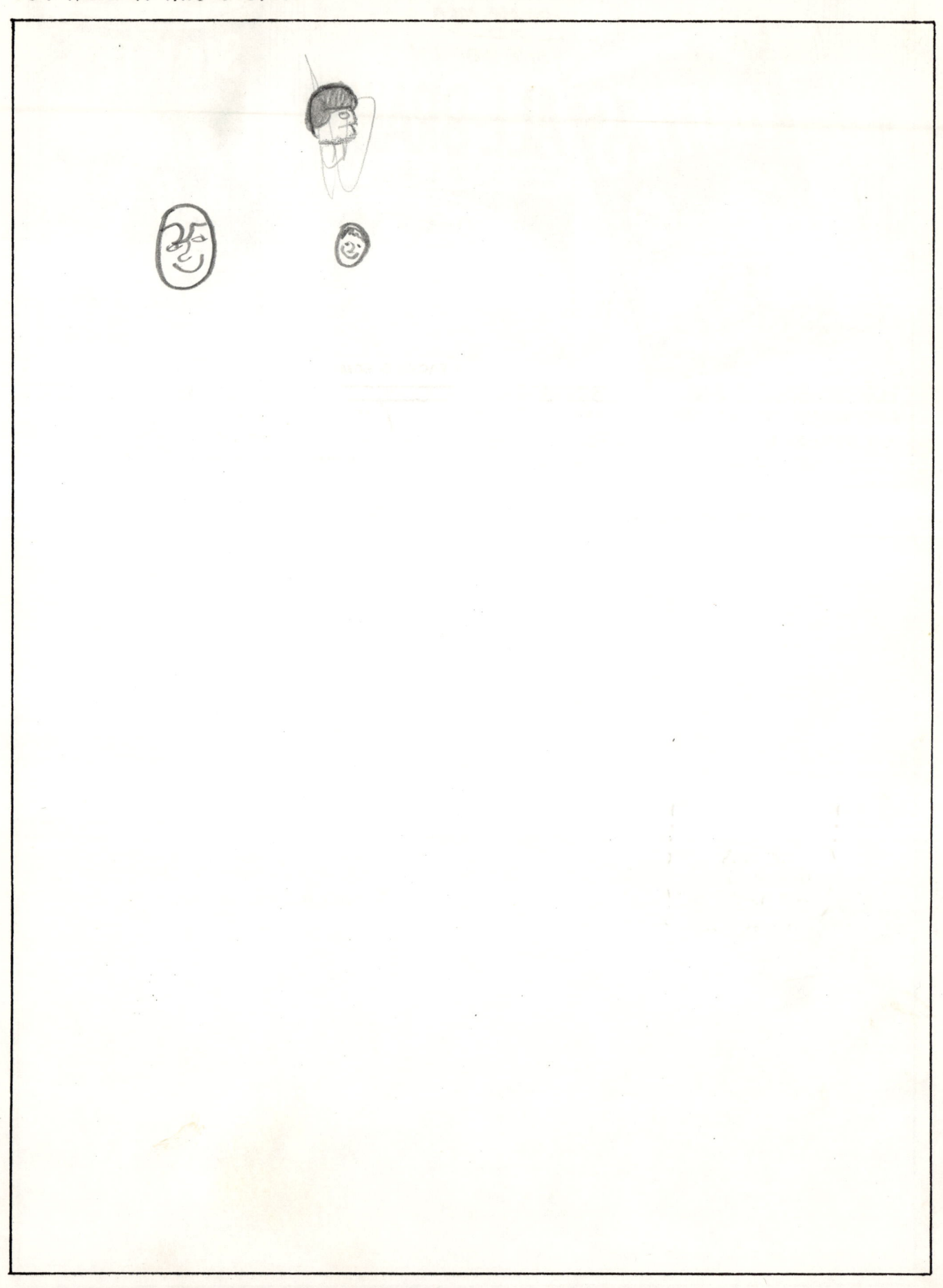

DRAW YOUR OWN FATHER AND SON CHARACTERS - THEN NAME THEM AND PUT THEM IN THIS STORY...

LETTER THE NAME OF YOUR COMIC

Fishing

"ARE YOU READY FOR OUR FISHING TRIP?"

"ALMOST, DAD! I JUST HAVE TO PACK ONE MORE THING."

DAD AND SON ARE GETTING READY TO GO FISHING — SON IS PACKING SOMETHING IN SUITCASE.

"WHAT'S THAT?"

"MY MAGNIFYING GLASS — SO THE *FISH YOU CATCH* WILL LOOK *BIGGER!*"

DAD LOOKS AS SON HOLDS UP MAGNIFYING GLASS.

"I HAVE A HUNCH THE FISH ARE BITING TODAY!"

"I HOPE SO, DAD! THE ONLY THING YOU CAUGHT LAST TIME WAS A **BAD COLD**!"

BOTH WALKING ON DOCK TO GO FISHING.

Panel 1:

"GOLLY! WOW!! I THINK I HOOKED ONE, DAD!"

"PULL IT IN! PULL IT IN!!"

THEY ARE BOTH FISHING OFF A PIER.

Panel 2:

"AW..... IT'S JUST A TIRE!"

"HA-HA! THROW IT BACK, SON. IT'S TOO SMALL FOR OUR CAR!"

SON HAS HOOKED A TIRE ON HIS LINE.

Panel 3:

"JUMPING-JELLY-BEANS!! ANOTHER BITE! LOOK AT THAT POLE BEND!!! IT MUST BE JAWS!!"

SONS POLE IS BENT- HE HAS HOOKED SOMETHING ELSE.

Panel 1:

"OH, NUTS! NUTTY NUTS!! AN OLD BUCKET!!"

"HA-HA! YOU'RE REALLY CATCHING THEM TODAY!!"

SON HAS PULLED UP AN OLD BUCKET

Panel 2:

"DAD!! LOOK!! A BIG FISH WAS IN THE BUCKET!"

"WOW! IT'S A BEAUTY!"

SON POINTS TO BUCKET- LARGE FISH COMES OUT OF IT.

Panel 3:

"HERE'S YOUR $100.00 PRIZE!"

"100 DOLLARS! THAT'S A LOT OF FINS FOR A FEW FINS!"

JUDGE HANDS SON PRIZE MONEY - DAD WATCHING.

THE END

BECOME A COMIC INVENTOR —

POLICE BADGES THAT DO SOME GOOD

GUITAR FOR ROMANTIC TYPE SINGERS

RING LIGHTS FOR NEWLY ENGAGED GIRLS

PENCIL THAT DOESN'T GET SHARPENED DOWN TO A STUB IN A HURRY

ICE CREAM CONES THAT DON'T DRIP ON NEAT LITTLE GIRLS

COMIC INVENTIONS

by — Jake Bomig

a set of markers that won't run out fast, 24 diffrent colors, 240 different markers.

THERE IS NEVER ONE AROUND WHEN YOU NEED IT!

THESE TWO COMICS ARE ABOUT THINGS THAT HAPPEN AROUND YOU — *NEVER A TAXI* — *ALWAYS LATE TRAIN*. ON THE NEXT PAGE DRAW A COMIC OF SOMETHING THAT ALWAYS HAPPENS AROUND YOU. BREAK UP THE PAGE INTO AS MANY PANELS AS YOU NEED TO TELL YOUR STORY.

DEPENDABLY UNDEPENDABLE!

- LOOKS LIKE THE 7:46 IS GOING TO BE LATE — BY TWO DAYS!
- IF THIS WAS A MILK TRAIN, THE MILK WOULD BE BUTTER BY NOW.
- YESTERDAY I GOT INTO THE OFFICE SO LATE THAT I MISSED THREE COFFEE BREAKS!
- I HEAR THE ENGINEER ON THIS LINE IS RELATED TO RIP VAN WINKLE.
- LAST NIGHT I GOT HOME SO LATE THAT MY WIFE SERVED ME SOMETHING NEW... *TV BREAKFAST!*

WHAT WILL SUSIE AND SAM FIND? IT'S UP TO YOU — THEY CAN FIND *HIDDEN TREASURE* — A *SPACE MAN* — A *LOST COW* — A *TALKING CAT* — A *LEPRECHAUN* — A *GIANT*? ANYTHING THAT YOU WANT THEM TO FIND THEY WILL! ALL YOU HAVE TO DO IS CONTINUE THIS STORY ON THE NEXT FEW PAGES AND DRAW THE PICTURES.

BENJAMIN FRANKLIN

"THAT TIME-MACHINE WAS NO JOKE!"

DRAW A COMIC ABOUT 2 CHILDREN WHO FIND A TIME MACHINE.

DRAW A COMIC ABOUT JULIUS CAESAR WHEN HE WAS A LITTLE BOY.

LITTLE CAESAR

"HAIL, CAESAR!"

"NO, JUST A LITTLE RAIN!"

NOW THAT YOU'VE COMPLETED THIS BOOK, I'D LIKE VERY MUCH TO SEE ONE OF YOUR COMICS — COULD YOU SEND ME ONE?
     THANKYOU —
TONY TALLARICO
c/o GROSSET & DUNLAP,
51 MADISON AVE.,
N.Y., N.Y. 10010

tallarico